The Sayings of D.H. Lawrence

The Sayings of

D. H. LAWRENCE

edited by

Stoddard Martin

DUCKWORTH

for Jane Corbett,
who introduced me to Lawrence,
Leavis and a robust English tradition of self-criticism

First published in 1995 by
Gerald Duckworth & Co. Ltd.
The Old Piano Factory
48 Hoxton Square, London N1 6PB
Tel: 0171 729 5986
Fax: 0171 729 0015

Introduction and editorial arrangement
© 1995 by Stoddard Martin

A catalogue record for this book is available
from the British Library

ISBN 0 7156 2639 6

Typeset by Ray Davies
Printed in Great Britain by
Redwood Books Ltd., Trowbridge

Contents

A Note on the Text

In extracting these sayings, it has sometimes been useful to delete a repetitious phrase or irrelevancy, or to alter the tense of a verb. Nowhere has there been any alteration of sense or replacement of Lawrence's actual words.

When the quotation is from the speech of a character in a novel, his or her name has been noted. However, when the quotation is narrated in the third person from the point of view of a focal character, no notation is made.

Introduction

D.H. Lawrence is one of those exceptionally well-known writers about whom so much has been said that to rehearse the facts of his life (1885-1930) might be to waste the time even of those whose knowledge of literature extends no further than TV costume-dramas. Interest in Lawrence has in any case usually been less in the facts than in journalistic sound-bytes: he was a sexist, a racist, a prophet, a pornographer, a 'priest of love', a demon, a pathetic amalgamation of working-class bully and wimp, and so on. Each of these versions has provided a nice revelation of its makers, as of Lawrence himself. Like Byron or Nietzsche or Freud, his name has become a symbol or slogan. As with them, one suspects that many of those who refer to him knowingly nowadays have not read more than a few juicy bits of his voluminous opus.

To the English academic literary establishment of the post-War period, F.R. Leavis notably, Lawrence was one of 'our' greatest novelists. His heartfelt, autobiographical fictions of struggle up from a Midlands mining town background were held out as an essential part of the canon of their time. His naturalistic pictures of a social and psychological milieu, while hardly innovative stylistically, were extolled for their detail and passion. A particular talent for description of flowers marked him out as an inheritor of the tradition of Wordsworth and Hardy. A Rousseauesque radicalism congenial to the antinomian generation of the 1960s secured him status as a heroic precursor up to and following the obscenity trial of *Lady Chatterley's Lover*.

Less commonly noted by English enthusiasts was that within a few years of his elopement with Frieda von Richthofen in 1912, Lawrence turned his back on his country. His great novel *Women in Love*, written during the First World War but prevented from release until

1921, marked the end of his identity as the prose-poet of the Midlands and beginning of a coruscating 'goodbye to all that'. The authorities' harassment of him as a pacifist and of Frieda as a suspected spy contributed to his disillusionment. But it was not just that which prompted Lawrence's acidulous tone. Nor did his animus abate through his subsequent wanderings, though some nostalgia for his homeland appears in the one great late novel placed in an English setting – *Lady Chatterley* again.

What did Lawrence have against the England of his day? First, he believed in the old Romantic notion that the Industrial Revolution had been a fatal wrong turn: the 'green and pleasant land' was now rotten with a soulless, petty urbanism and the money ethic. On a more personal level, he felt damaged by a social order and climate which had given him a class handicap, a patchy education and tubercular lungs. Some may rationalise Lawrence's castigations of England as projections of his peculiar shortcomings, but this would be no more prudent than to dismiss Nietzsche's censure of Germany a few decades before as a result of syphilis. Like Nietzsche's, Lawrence's hypersensitivity enabled him to see a cultural crisis brewing which would bring change in all areas of national life, from the most public to the most private. The latter led to his principal identification for posterity: with the revolt against Victorian prudery.

At the first opportunity after the end of the War, Lawrence and Frieda escaped to the Continent. Initially they went to Italy, where they had been happy during their original elopement. Soon, however, they were voyaging restlessly to Ceylon, Australia, Mexico, New Mexico, Europe again – Germany and England briefly – back to the Americas, back to Italy and finally to the south of France. These wanderings took on a semi-metaphysical purpose: a quest for the Lawrentian version of Henry James's 'great good place'. The sun, however, was the principal beacon for Lawrence, not a higher social order. Health demanded the south; prejudice and pride dictated avoidance of 'overcivilised' climes. In this Lawrence was at one with a larger turning in his generation from the decadence of old Europe toward a revitalising primitivism.

Lawrence's wanderings have been described as a journey within, into the 'dark soul' of the self. Certainly they deepened and hardened the 'figure on the carpet' for him: the vaguely Luddite hostility to technological advances; the view that men and women had become progressively debased and out of touch with their 'passional' cores. The truth is that when Lawrence could view humans as manifestations of Nature, like flowers or serpents, he was fascinated by them; but when he was asked to enter into extended relations with them, he recoiled, fearful that they might disturb the essential singleness in him and sap his mercurial vitality – a sad yet no doubt accurate perception.

A fatal misanthropy grows more apparent: a Nietzschean rejection of the 'human, all too human' and desire for man (not least himself) to be transformed into something more potent and godly. Thus we have the *Zarathustra*-like dithyrambs to 'phallic consciousness' which run through the works of his so called 'dark period', leading up to and including his most ideological novel, *The Plumed Serpent*. As with Nietzsche's hybrid 'transformational' book, from which it derives, Lawrence's most extensive attempt to evoke a new religion was written in a white heat in a phase of amorous and existential crisis around his fortieth year. And, as with Nietzsche, the strain of composition increased his ill-health and alienation to such a pitch that he never fully recovered.

Critics generally see the Lawrence of the later years as inferior to the hopeful young novelist of *Sons and Lovers* and *The Rainbow*. But Lawrence had long since left behind the desire to write conventional fiction; and the advent of philosophising in his work provides us with its most noteworthy sayings. Like those of the later Nietzsche, these Lawrentian *aperçus* demonstrate a brilliance which sometimes borders on the crazed. The fight against TB, like Nietzsche's fight against syphilis, runs as an undercurrent always threatening to rise up and engulf common sense, like the floodwaters of the river which inundate the old order of sick England at the end of *The Virgin and the Gypsy* – a posthumously-published book which, along with others such as *Apocalypse*, signals an identity to the end between Lawrence's views and the decay of his body.

I have compared Lawrence with Nietzsche, but his emblematic short life resembles those of many others in the last phase of Romanticism. Baudelaire and Wilde also met crisis and death in their mid-forties after having lived as *voyants*, moral rebels and forerunners of the sexual revolution of our century. And there is a certain poetic justice that they all 'passed beyond our view' when they did: as Lawrence's friend Aldous Huxley pointed out, this type of writer has most to offer to the young and virile. The spectacle of living on into feebleness could have little mythic value for leading lights in an era of writer-as-hero. Nor could a vitalist anti-Christ advance his cause by becoming a Mosaic grey-beard, any more than by collapsing at the foot of the cross of a God with whom he may have identified but in whom he could no longer believe.

In Lawrence's case, this deficiency – that he has little to offer for the weak, the old or even the middle-aged – may hasten the decline of his reputation in an era of increasingly 'grey' populations. Already one can foresee the day when he will become a marginal figure in England, as he has long been on the Continent; indeed, it may be left to the youth-oriented sun-culture of the American southwest (a place which he liked and perhaps understood better than most) to preserve his memory as one of 'our' truly great writers. Meanwhile, for those who inhabit less parochial regions of culture, Lawrence should retain permanent interest for his insights into a new age being born in relations between men and women and in essential religion.

Civilisation & Politics

One must destroy the spirit of money, the blind spirit of
possession ... The only permanent thing is *consummation* in
love or hate.   Letter to Lady Cynthia Asquith, 1915

When the peasant suddenly leaves his home and becomes a
workman, an entire change comes over everywhere. Life is
now a matter of selling oneself to slave-work, building roads
or labouring in quarries or mines or on the railways,
purposeless, meaningless ... It seems as though we should be
left at last with a great system of roads and railways and
industries, and a world of utter chaos seething upon these
fabrications.   *Twilight in Italy*, 1916

The poor dear old ship of Christian democracy is scuttled at
last, the breach is made, the veil of the temple is torn, our
epoch is over. *Soit!* I don't care, it's not my doing, and I can't
help it. It isn't a question of 'dancing while Rome burns' ... It is
a question of bobbing about gaily in the chaos.
                              Letter to Cynthia Asquith, 1916

All this talk of war, this talk of nationality, to me is false. I feel
no nationality, not fundamentally. I feel no passion for my own
land, nor my own house, nor my own furniture, nor my own
money. Therefore I won't pretend any. Neither will I take part
in the scrimmage, to help my neighbour. It is his affair to go in
or to stay out.
                              Letter to Catherine Carswell, 1916

Fusty, fuzzy peace cranks and lovers of humanity are the devil.
We must get on a new track altogether. Damn Humanity, let
me have a bit of inhuman, or non human truth, that our fuzzy
human emotions can't alter.
                              Letter to Cynthia Asquith, 1916

Politics – what are they? Just another, extra large, commercial
wrangle over buying and selling – nothing else.
                                          'Democracy', 1917

The question of property will never be settled till people cease
to care for property. Then it will settle itself.   *Ibid.*

The prime minister of the future will be no more than a sort of steward.   *Ibid.*

The old world must burst, the underworld must be open and a whole, new world [emerge] ... an emotional sensuous underworld ... an ecstatic, subtly intellectual underworld, like the Greeks – Orphicism – like Magdalene at her feet washing.
Letter to Cecil Gray, 1918

If only one could be an animal, with a thick warm hide, and never a stitch or rag besides. Nobody ought to own houses or furniture – any more than they own the stones of the high road.
Ibid.

Could anything be more *infra dig* than the performing of a set of special actions day in day out, for a lifetime, in order to receive some shillings every seventh day? ... Far better be a slave outright, in contact with all the whims and impulses of a human being, than serve some mechanical routine of modern work.   *The Lost Girl*, 1920

I want every man to have his share in the world's goods, so that I am rid of his importunity, so that I can tell him: 'Now you've got what you want ... Now, you one-mouthed fool, mind yourself and don't obstruct me.'
Women in Love, 1921 (Birkin)

If I knew how to, I'd really join myself to the revolutionary socialists now. I think the time has come for a real struggle. I don't care for politics. But I know there must and should be a deadly revolution very soon.
Letter to Eleanor Farjeon, 1921

A reaction is setting in, away from the old universality, back, away from cosmopolitanism and internationalism ... I shall be glad when men hate their common, world alike clothes, when they tear them up and clothe themselves fiercely for distinction, savage distinction.   *Sea and Sardinia*, 1921

Endless pity for the ignorant. It is only slackness. The pity makes the ignorant more ignorant ... What they need is not pity but prods.   *Ibid.*

The world fears a new experience more than it fears anything.
Studies in Classic American Literature, 1923 (Spirit of Place)

In the new epoch that is coming, there will be no letter of the
law.   *Ibid.* (Cooper)

The machine is the great neuter. It is the eunuch of eunuchs. In
the end it emasculates us all.   *Ibid.* (Dana)

We know enough. We know too much. We know nothing. Let
us smash something. Ourselves included. But the machine
above all.   *Ibid.* (Dana)

Far be it from me to assume any 'white' superiority.
                                                 Ibid. (Melville)

Beyond all the ashy pallor and sulphur of our civilisation, lurks
the great blood creature waiting, implacable and eternal, ready
at last to crush out our white brittleness and let the shadowy
blood move erect once more, in a new implacable pride and
strength.   'The Border Line', 1924

History is the account of a lesson which nobody ever learns.
                                             'None of That', 1924

There is no break in the great adventure in consciousness.
Throughout the howlingest deluge, some few brave souls are
steering the ark under the rainbow ... Man is an adventurer,
and he must never give up the adventure.   'Books', 1924

Nothing matters, but that strange flame, of inborn nobility that
obliges men to be brave, and onward plunging.
                                                 St Mawr, 1925

Our whole civilisation is nasty minded as eunuchs are, with
their kind of sneaking, sterilising cruelty.   *Ibid.*

The world is made up of a mass of people and a few
individuals.   *The Plumed Serpent*, 1926

There are only two great diseases in the world today –
Bolshevism and Americanism; and Americanism is the worse
of the two, because Bolshevism only smashes your house or
your business or your skull, but Americanism smashes your
soul.   *Ibid.* (Henry)

Let us defend ourselves from the bottom dog, with its mean
growl and its yellow teeth.   *Ibid.*

Bolshevists, somehow, seem to be born on the railway. Wherever the iron rails run, and passengers are hauled back and forth in railway coaches, there the spirit of rootlessness, of transitoriness, of first and second class in separate compartments, of envy and malice, and of iron and demonish panting engines, seems to bring forth the logical children of materialism.   *Ibid.*

It is the cold, collective lust of millions of people, to break the spirit in the outstanding individuals ... so that they can start the great downhill rush back to the old underworld levels, old gold worship and murder lust.   *Ibid.*

Panic and murder never start unless the leading people let slip the control.   *Ibid.* (Kate)

The world has gone as far as it can in the good, gentle, and loving direction, and anything farther in that line means perversity.   *Ibid.*

The surest way to kill the new spirit – and it can be killed, like any other living thing – is to get it connected with any political party.   *Ibid.* (Don Ramón)

Only the Natural Aristocrats can rise above their nation; and even then they do not rise beyond their race.

Ibid. (Don Ramón)

Only the man of a great star, a great divinity, can bring the opposites together again, in a new unison.   *Ibid.*

The great white monkey has got hold of the keys of the world.
Mornings in Mexico, 1927

To carry on a tradition you must add something to the tradition. But to keep up a convention needs only the monotonous persistency of a parasite, the endless endurance of the craven, those who fear life, because they are not alive, and who cannot die because they cannot live – the social beings.
'John Galsworthy', 1927

If there is one thing more repulsive than the social being positive, it is the social being negative ... In the great debacle of decency this gentleman is the most indecent.   *Ibid.*

If life is a great highway, then it must forge ahead into the unknown. Sidetracking gets nowhere: that is mere *anti*. The tip of the road is always unfinished, in the wilderness.

Ibid.

The dead materialism of Marx socialism and soviets seems to me no better than what we've got. What we want is life and trust; men trusting men, and making living a free thing, not a thing to be *earned*. Letter to Charles Wilson, 1928

While men are courageous and willing to change, nothing terribly bad can happen. But once men fall into a state of funk, with the inevitable accompaniment of bullying and repression, then only bad things can happen … Bullying of any sort whatsoever can have nothing but disastrous results.

'The State of Funk', 1928

Ours is essentially a tragic age, so we refuse to take it tragically. The cataclysm has happened, we are among the ruins, we start to build up new little habitats, to have new little hopes. It is rather hard work: there is now no smooth road into the future; but we go round, or scramble over the obstacles. We've got to live, no matter how many skies have fallen.

Lady Chatterley's Lover, 1928

All the great words are cancelled for our generation: love, joy, happiness, home, mother, father, husband, all these great, dynamic words are half dead now, and dying from day to day … All that remains is a certain stubborn stoicism; and in that there is a certain pleasure. *Ibid.*

There is only one class nowadays: moneyboys. The moneyboy and the moneygirl, the only difference is how much you've got, and how much you want.

Ibid.

A man can no longer be private and withdrawn. The world allows no hermits. *Ibid.*

To keep industry alive there must be more industry, like a madness … And it requires a madman to succeed in it.

Ibid.

Oh, the joy hogs! Oh 'enjoying oneself'! Another modern form of sickness.

Ibid.

There's a bad time coming ... If things go on as they are, there's nothing in the future but death and destruction, for these industrial masses ... But never mind. All the bad times that ever have been, haven't been able to blow the crocus out.

Ibid. (Mellors)

One may be at war with society, and still keep one's deep peace with mankind.

'Nobody Loves Me', 1929

The love of humanity is gone, leaving a great gap. The cosmic consciousness has collapsed upon a great void. The egoist sits grinning furtively in the triumph of his own emptiness.

Ibid.

Ours is an excessively conscious age. We know so much, we feel so little.

'Making Pictures', 1929

Never was an age more sentimental, more devoid of real feeling, more exaggerated in fake feeling than our own.

'A Propos of *Lady Chatterley's Lover*',1930

The radio and the film are mere counterfeit emotion all the time, the current press and literature the same. People wallow in emotion: counterfeit emotion. They lap it up: they live in and on it. They ooze with it.

Ibid.

Literature & Criticism

The literary world seems a particularly hateful yet powerful one. The literary element, like a disagreeable substratum under a fair country, spreads under every inch of life, sticking to the roots of the growing things. Ugh, that is hateful! I wish I might be delivered from it.

Letter to Helen Corke, 1910

If *Hamlet* and *Oedipus* were published now, they wouldn't sell more than 100 copies, unless they were pushed.

Letter to Edward Garnett, 1913

Every work of art adheres to some system of morality. But if it be really a work of art, it must contain the essential criticism on the morality to which it adheres ...

Study of Thomas Hardy, 1914

When an Englishman listens to a speech [in the theatre] he wants at least to imagine that he understands thoroughly and impersonally what is meant. But an Italian only cares about the emotion. It is the movement, the physical effect of the language upon the blood which gives him supreme satisfaction. His mind is scarcely engaged at all.

Twilight in Italy, 1916

Write for America if you can't write. I find I am unable to write for England any more – the response has gone quite dead and dumb. A certain hope rises in my heart, quite hot, and I can go on. But it is not England. It seems to me it is America. If I am kept here I am beaten for ever.

Letter to Catherine Carswell, 1917

Any man of real individuality tries to know and to understand what is happening, even in himself, as he goes along. This struggle for verbal consciousness should not be left out in art. It is a very great part of life. It is not superimposition of a theory. It is the passionate struggle into conscious being.

Women in Love, 1921 (Foreword)

One shouldn't talk when one is tired. One Hamletizes, and it seems a lie.   *Ibid.* (Birkin)

I must remember again Oscar Wilde ... What a terrible mistake, to let oneself be martyred by a lot of *canaille*. A man must say his say. But *noli me tangere*.

Sea and Sardinia, 1921

Reading other people's books is better than having to read one's own: and it's much better to be doing something than nothing.   Letter to Cynthia Asquith, 1922

The trouble with realism is that the writer, when he is a truly exceptional man like Flaubert, tries to read his own sense of tragedy into people much smaller than himself.

'Giovanni Verga', 1922

The great tragic soul of Shakespeare borrows the bodies of kings and princes – not out of snobbism, but out of natural affinity. You can't put a great soul into a commonplace person.

Ibid.

The realistic-democratic age has dodged the dilemma of having no heroes by having every man his own hero. This is reached by what we call subjective intensity.

Ibid.

When a man writes a letter to himself, it is a pity to post it to somebody else. Perhaps the same is true of a book.

Aaron's Rod, 1922

The European moderns are all *trying* to be extreme. The great Americans just were it.

Studies in Classic American Literature, 1923 (Spirit of Place)

Shakespeare's whole tragic wail is because of the downfall of the true male authority, the ithyphallic authority and masterhood. It fell with Elizabeth. It was trodden underfoot with Victoria.   *Ibid.* (Hawthorne)

What happens when you idealise the soil, the mother-earth, and really go back to it? Then with overwhelming conviction it is borne in upon you, as it was upon Thomas Hardy, that the whole scheme of things is against you.

Ibid. (Dana)

What a man has got to say is never more than relatively
important. To kill yourself like Keats, for what you've got to
say, is to mix the eggshell in with the omlette.

> Letter to Middleton Murry, 1926

In the real summer, I always lose interest in literature and
publications.

> Letter to Martin Secker, 1926

Why do any more books? There are so many, and such a small
demand for what there are. So why add to the burden, and
waste one's vitality over it.

> *Ibid.*

A critic must be able to *feel* the impact of a work of art in all its
complexity and its force. To do so, he must be a man of force
and complexity himself, which few critics are. A man with a
paltry, impudent nature will never write anything but paltry,
impudent criticism. And a man who is *emotionally* educated is
as rare as a phoenix.

> 'John Galsworthy', 1927

Satire exists for the very purpose of killing the social being,
showing him what an inferior he is and, with all his parade of
social honesty, how subtly and corruptly debased … By
ridiculing the social being, the satirist helps the true individual,
the real human being, to rise to his feet again.

> *Ibid.*

[*Lady Chatterley's Lover*] is the most important novel ever
written and you would probably find it pure pornography. But
it isn't. It's a declaration of the phallic reality.

> Letter to S.S. Koteliansky, 1927

Goethe *began* million of intimacies, and never got beyond the
how-do-you-do stage, then fell off into his own boundless ego.
He perverted himself into perfection and God-likeness.

> Letter to Aldous Huxley, 1928

My God, what a clumsy *olla putrida* James Joyce is! nothing but
old fags and cabbage-stumps of quotations from the Bible and
the rest, stewed in the juice of deliberate, journalistic
dirty-mindedness – what old and hard-worked staleness,
masquerading as the all-new! Gertrude Stein is more amusing.

> Letter to Maria and Aldous Huxley, 1928

As a novelist, I feel it is the change inside the individual which is my real concern. The great social change interests me and troubles me, but it is not my field ... My field is to know the feelings inside a man, and to make new feelings conscious.

'The State of Funk', 1928

It is the way our sympathy flows and recoils that really determines our lives. And here lies the vast importance of the novel properly handled. It can inform and lead into new places the flow of our sympathetic consciousness, and it can lead our sympathy away in recoil from things gone dead ... It is in the *passional* secret places of life, above all, that the tide of sensitive awareness needs to ebb and flow, cleansing and refreshing.

Lady Chatterley's Lover, 1928

The novel, like gossip, can also excite spurious sympathies and recoils, mechanical and deadening to the psyche. [It] can glorify the most corrupt feelings, so long as they are *conventionally* 'pure'. Then the novel, like gossip, becomes at last vicious, and, like gossip, all the more vicious because it is always ostensibly on the side of the angels.

Ibid.

The public responds now only to an appeal to its vices.

Ibid.

I would censor genuine pornography, vigorously ... You can recognise it by the insult it offers, invariably, to sex and to the human spirit ... Obscenity only comes in when the mind despises and fears the body.

'Pornography and Obscenity', 1929

A book lives as long as it is unfathomed. Once it is fathomed, it dies.

Apocalypse, 1930

It is far, far better to read one book six times, at intervals, than to read six several books.

Ibid.

Art & Aesthetics

Art which knows the struggle between the two conflicting laws [of male and female], and knows the final reconciliation, where both are equal, two in one, complete, is the supreme art. Some men have attempted it, and left us the results of their efforts. But it remains to be done.

Study of Thomas Hardy, 1914

The secret, shameful things are most terribly beautiful.
The Rainbow, 1915

Art should *interpret* industry as art once interpreted religion.
Women in Love, 1921 (Loerke)

The past and the future are the two great bournes of human emotion. They are both conclusive, final. Their beauty is the beauty of the goal, finished, perfected.
New Poems, 1920 (Preface)

The ideal – what is the ideal? A figment. An abstraction. A fragment of the before or the after ... a crystallized aspiration, or a crystallized remembrance: crystallized, set, finished.
Ibid.

Never trust the artist. Trust the tale. The proper function of a critic is to save the tale from the artist who created it.
Studies in Classic American Literature, 1923 (Spirit of Place)

You can idealize or intellectualize. Or, on the contrary, you can let the dark soul in you see for itself. An artist usually intellectualizes on top, and his dark under-consciousness goes on contradicting him beneath.
Ibid. (de Crèvecoeur)

If there is one thing that annoys me more than a business man and his BUSINESS, it is an artist, a writer, painter, musician, and MY WORK. When an artist says MY WORK, the flesh goes tired on my bones.
Ibid. (Cooper)

In true art there is always the double rhythm of creating and destroying.
Ibid. (Poe)

The essential function of art is moral. Not aesthetic, not decorative, not pastime and recreation. But a passionate, implicit morality, not didactic. A morality which changes the blood first. The mind follows later.

Ibid. (Whitman)

About daubing paint on canvas: every possible daub that can be daubed has already been done, so people ought to leave off.
St Mawr, 1925 (Lou)

Beauty is a mystery. You can neither eat it nor make flannel out of it.

'Sex versus Loveliness', 1928

Science has a mysterious hatred of beauty, because it doesn't fit in the cause-and-effect chain.   *Ibid.*

To love living beauty you must have a reverence for sex.

Ibid.

Sex and beauty are inseparable, like life and consciousness.

Ibid.

The intelligence which goes with sex and beauty, and arises out of sex and beauty, is intuition.

Ibid.

The plainest person can look beautiful, can *be* beautiful. It only needs the fire of sex to rise delicately to change an ugly face to a lovely one.   *Ibid.*

Nothing is more ugly than a human being in whom the fire of sex has gone out.   *Ibid.*

There are all kinds of beauty in the world, thank God ... Ugliness is homogeneous.

'New Mexico', 1928

When passion is dead, or absent, then the magnificent throb of beauty is incomprehensible and even a little despicable ... warm, live beauty of contact, so much deeper than the beauty of vision.   *Lady Chatterley's Lover*, 1928

The human soul needs actual beauty even more than bread.
'Nottingham and the Mining Country',1929

What we want is a bigger gesture, a greater scope, a certain splendour, a certain grandeur, and beauty, big beauty. The American does far better than us, in this.

Ibid.

The most exciting moment [is] when you have a blank canvas and a big brush full of wet colour, and you plunge.

'Making Pictures', 1929

The modern theories of art make real pictures impossible.

Ibid.

An artist may be a profligate and, from a social point of view, a scoundrel. But if he can paint a nude woman, or a couple of apples, so that they are a living image, then he is pure in spirit.

Ibid.

Art is treated all wrong ... as if it were a science, which it is not. Art is a form of religion, minus the Ten Commandments business, which is sociological.

Ibid.

A model only spoils the picture. The picture must all come out of the artist's inside, awareness of forms and figures ... It is more than memory. It is the image as it lives in the consciousness, alive like a vision, but unknown.

Ibid.

Teaching only hinders.   *Ibid.*

Blake is the only painter of imaginative pictures, apart from landscape, that England has produced.

The Paintings of D.H. Lawrence, 1929 (Introduction)

Landscape seems to be *meant* as a background to an intenser vision of life, so to my feeling painted landscape is background with the real subject left out.

Ibid.

An artist *can* only create what he really religiously *feels* is truth, religious truth, religious truth really *felt*, in the blood and the bones.

Ibid.

Some men can only get a vision by staring themselves blind, as it were: like Cezanne; but staring kills my vision ... The only thing one can look into, stare into, and see only vision, is the vision itself: the visionary image.

Ibid.

'Aesthetic ecstasy' sounds to me like another great uplift into self-importance, another apotheosis of personal conceit.

Ibid.

The history of our era is the nauseating and repulsive history of the crucifixion of the procreative body for the glorification of the spirit, the mental consciousness. Plato was the arch-priest of this crucifixion. Art, that handmaid, humbly and honestly served the vile deed, through three thousand years at least.   *Ibid.*

The gift of virtuosity simply means that you don't have to humble yourself, or even be honest with yourself, because you are a clever mental creature who is capable at will of making the intuitions and instincts subserve some mental concept.

Ibid.

Any creative act occupies the whole consciousness of a man. This is true of the great discoveries of science as well as of art.

Ibid.

The mind and the spirit alone can never really grasp a work of art, though they may, in a masturbating fashion, provoke the body into an ecstasized response. The ecstasy will die out into ash and more ash.

Ibid.

To a true artist, and to the living imagination, the cliché is the deadly enemy.

Ibid.

To introduce into our world of vision something which is neither optical nor mechanical nor intellectual-psychological requires a real revolution.

Ibid.

If innocence and naiveté as regards artistic expression doesn't become merely idiotic, why shouldn't it become ... a prelude to a golden age?

Ibid.

Love & Relationships

I ought not to blame women, as I have done, but myself, for taking my love to the wrong woman, before now. Let every man find, keep on trying till he finds, the woman who can take him and whose love he can take, then who will grumble about men or about women ... Oh, if people could only marry properly; I believe in marriage.

Letter to Mrs S.A. Hopkin, 1912

The establishment of a new relation, or the readjustment of the old one, between men and women, is *the* problem of today.

Letter to Edward Garnett, 1913

It is queer, but nobody seems to want, or to love, *two* people together. Heaps of folk love me alone – if I were alone – and of course all the world adores Frieda – when I'm not there. But together we seem to be a pest. I supposed married (*sic*) people ought to be sufficient to themselves.

Ibid.

Nothing is as bad as a marriage that's a hopeless failure.

Sons and Lovers, 1913 (Mrs Morel)

Love should give a sense of freedom, not of prison.

Ibid. (Paul)

One must learn to love, and go through a great deal of suffering to get to it, like any knight of the grail, and the journey is always *towards* the other soul, not away from it.

Letter to Sir Thomas Dunlop, 1914

To love, you have to understand the other, more than she understands herself, and to submit to her understanding of you. It is damnably difficult and painful, but it is the only thing which endures.

Ibid.

Passion is a very one-sided thing, based chiefly on hatred and *Wille zur Macht*.

Letter to Lady Ottoline Morrell, 1915

Passion is only part of love. And it seems so much because it can't last. That is why passion is never happy.

The Rainbow, 1915 (Ursula)

In marriage, husband and wife wage the subtle, satisfying war of sex upon each other. It gives a profound satisfaction, a profound intimacy. But it destroys all joy, all unanimity in action. *Twilight in Italy*, 1916

Pan and the ministers of Pan do not marry the sylvan gods. They are single and isolated in their being. It is in the spirit that marriage takes place. In the flesh there is connexion, but only in the spirit is there a new thing created out of two different antithetic beings ... an absolute, a Word. *Ibid.*

The undisputed reign of love can never be. Because love is strictly a travelling. 'Love', 1917

What worse bondage can we conceive than the bond of love? It is an attempt to wall in the high tide; it is a will to arrest the spring. *Ibid.*

There is a goal, but the goal is neither love nor death. It is a goal neither infinite nor eternal. It is the realm of calm delight, it is the other-kingdom of bliss. *Ibid.*

The point about love is that we hate the word because we have vulgarized it. It ought to be proscribed, tabooed from utterance, for many years, till we get a new, better idea.

Women in Love, 1921 (Birkin)

What I want is a strange conjunction ... not meeting and mingling ... but an equilibrium, a pure balance of two single beings: – as the stars balance each other.

Ibid. (Birkin)

To be free, in a free place, with a few other people! ... The perfect relation. *Ibid.* (Birkin)

Marriage in the old sense seems to me a sort of tacit hunting in couples: the world all in couples, each couple in its own little house, watching its own little interests, and stewing in its own little privacy – it's the most repulsive thing on earth ... One should avoid this *home* instinct. It's not an instinct, it's a habit of cowardliness. *Ibid.* (Birkin)

Those who die, and dying still can love, do not die. They live
still in the beloved. *Ibid.*

The fine old martial split between the sexes is tonic and
splendid ... Give me the old salty way of love. How I am
nauseated with sentiment and nobility, the macaroni
slithery-slobbery mess of modern adorations.

Sea and Sardinia, 1921

Love is a battle in which each party strives for the mastery of
the other's soul. So far, man has yielded the mastery to
woman. Now he is fighting for it back again. And too late, for
the woman will never yield.

Aaron's Rod, 1922 (Lilly)

Let there be clean and pure division first, perfected singleness.
That is the only way to final, living unison.

Ibid. (Lilly)

To fling down the whole soul in one gesture of finality in love
is as much a criminal suicide as to jump off a church tower or a
mountain peak. Let a man give himself as much as he likes in
love, to seven thousand extremities, he must never give
himself *away*. *Ibid.* (Lilly)

Women make fools of the spiritual men. And when, as men,
they've gone flop in their spirituality, they can't pick
themselves up whole any more. So they just crawl, and die
detesting the female, or the females, who made them fall.

Studies in Classic American Literature, 1923 (Hawthorne)

It is probable that men will have more than one wife, in the
coming America. *Ibid.* (Hawthorne)

Men live by food, but die if they eat too much. Men live by
love, but die, or cause death, if they love too much.

Ibid. (Poe)

It is love that causes the neuroticism of the day. It is love that is
the prime cause of tuberculosis ... A ghastly disease, love.

Ibid. (Poe)

In the end the desire for a 'perfect relationship' is just a vicious,
unmanly craving.

Ibid. (Melville)

All men find that you can't really merge in a woman, though you may go a long way. You can't manage the last bit. So you have to give it up, and try elsewhere if you *insist* on merging.
Ibid. (Whitman)

The high-road of Love is no Open Road. It is a narrow, tight way, where the soul walks hemmed in between compulsions.
Ibid. (Whitman)

Beyond all race is the problem of man and woman.
'The Border Line', 1924

What nonsense it all is, this being-in-love business.
'The Last Laugh', 1924

Ever since men and women were men and women, people who took things seriously, and had time for it, got their hearts broken.
St Mawr, 1925

Men and women have really hurt one another so much, nowadays, that they had better stay apart till they have learned to be gentle with one another again. Not all this forced passion and destructive philandering.
Ibid. (Lou)

A woman who isn't quite ordinary herself can only love a man who is fighting for something beyond the ordinary life.
The Plumed Serpent, 1926 (Kate)

A woman who just wants to be taken, and then cling on, is a parasite. And a man who wants just to take, without giving, is a creature of prey.
Ibid. (Don Ramón)

With a woman a man always wants to let himself go. And it is precisely with a woman that he should never let himself go.
Ibid. (Don Ramón)

A man only betrays because he has been given a *part*, and not the whole. And a woman only betrays because only the part has been taken from her, and not the whole.
Ibid. (Teresa)

Women must be soldiers in spirit, and they need soldier husbands.
Ibid. (Teresa)

Many women play with love and intimacy as a cat with a mouse. In the end, they quickly eat up the love mouse, then trot off with a full belly and a voluptuous sense of power. Only sometimes the love-mouse refuses to be digested, and there is life-long dyspepsia. Or turns into a sort of serpent, that rears and looks at her with glittering eyes, then slides away into the void, leaving her blank … One after another, the powerful love-women, at the age of forty, forty-five, fifty, they all lose their charm and allure, and turn into real grimalkins, greyish, avid, and horrifying, prowling around looking for prey that becomes scarcer and scarcer. As human beings they go to pieces. And they remain these grey-ribbed grimalkins, dressed in elegant clothes, the grimalkin howl even passing into their smart chatter.

Ibid. (Kate)

A man has to be in love in his thighs, the way you ride a horse. Why don't we stay in love that way all our lives? Why do we turn into corpses with consciousness?

'Glad Ghosts', 1926

Nothing is so awful as a man who has fallen in love … So doggy!

'In Love', 1927

Why don't men marry the women who would really adore them?

Lady Chatterley's Lover, 1928 (Connie)

Perhaps only people who are capable of real togetherness have that look of being alone in the universe … The others have a certain stickiness, they stick to the mass.

Ibid. (Connie)

To yield entirely to love would be to be absorbed, which is the death of the individual … So we see that what our age has proved to its astonishment and dismay is that the individual *cannot* love … It is not that each man kills the thing he loves, but that each man, by insisting on his own individuality, kills the lover in himself.

Apocalypse, 1930

Sex & the Sexes

The act, called the sexual act, is not for the depositing of seed. It is for leaping off into the unknown.

Study of Thomas Hardy, 1914

A real 'man' takes no heed for his body, which is the more female part of him. He considers himself only as an instrument, to be used in the service of some idea. The true female, on the other hand, will eternally hold herself superior to any idea, will hold life in the body to be the real happiness.

Ibid.

The womb is full of darkness and also flooded with the strange white light of eternity. 'The Crown', 1915

The woman in her maternity is the law-giver, the supreme authority. The authority of the man, in work, in public affairs, is something trivial in comparison.

Twilight in Italy, 1916

Man is a queer beast. He spends dozens of centuries puffing himself up and drawing himself in, and at last he has to be content to be just his own size, neither infinitely big nor infinitely little. Man is tragi-comical.

'Democracy', 1917

Sex is such a limitation. It is sex that turns a man into a broken half of a couple, the woman into the other broken half.

Women in Love, 1921

There are great mysteries to be unsealed, sensual, mindless, dreadful mysteries, far beyond the phallic cult.

Ibid.

Why *does* every woman think her aim in life is to have a hubby and a little grey home in the west? Why is this the goal of life? Why should it be? *Ibid.* (Ursula)

How beautiful maleness is, if it finds its right expression. – And how perfectly ridiculous it is made in modern clothes.

Sea and Sardinia, 1921

One realises, with horror, that the race of men is almost extinct in Europe. Only Christ-like heroes and woman-worshipping Don Juans, and rabid equality-mongrels.

Ibid.

Men who can be quietly kind and simple to a woman, without wanting to show off or to make an impression are men still … neither humble nor conceited.

Ibid.

Woman will sacrifice eleven men, fathers, husbands, brothers and lovers, for one baby – or for her own female self-conceit.

Aaron's Rod, 1922 (Lilly)

Can you find two men to stick together, without feeling criminal, and without cringing, and without betraying one another? You can't. One is sure to go fawning round some female; then they both enjoy giving each other away, and doing a new grovel before a woman again.

Ibid. (Lilly)

Woman must be loved and adored, and above all, obeyed: particularly in her sex desire. There she must not be thwarted, or she becomes a devil. And if she is obeyed, she becomes a misunderstood woman with nerves, looking round for the next man whom she can bring under. So it is.

Ibid. (Marchese del Torre)

Let a woman loose from the bounds and restraints of man's fierce belief, in his gods and in himself, and she becomes a gentle devil.

Studies in Classic American Literature, 1923 (Hawthorne)

REVENGE! It is this that fills the unconscious spirit of woman today. Revenge against man, and against the spirit of man which has betrayed her into unbelief.

Ibid. (Hawthorne)

The one enduring thing a woman can have, the intangible soft flood of contentment that carries her along at the side of the man she is married to. It is her perfection and her highest attainment.

'The Border Line', 1924

I couldn't give my body to any woman who didn't respect it.

St Mawr, 1925 (Lewis)

Sex, mere sex, is repellant to me.   *Ibid.* (Lou)

She [the heroine] did not want to mate with a house-dog.
The Virgin and the Gypsy, 1925

All a man's hope, his honour, his faith, his trust, his belief in
life and creation and God, all these things can come to a crisis
in the moment of coition.

The Plumed Serpent, 1926

There is no liberty for a man, apart from the God of his
manhood.   *Ibid.* (Don Ramón)

The instriking thud of a heavy knife, stabbing into a living
body, is the inevitable supreme gratification of a people
entangled in the past, and unable to extricate itself. No lust of
women can equal this lust.

Ibid.

Sex is a powerful, potent thing not to be played with or
paraded. The one mystery. And a mystery greater than the
individual. The individual hardly counts.

Ibid.

If women thieve the world's virility, it is only because men
want to have it thieved, since for men to be responsible for
their own manhood seems to be the last thing men want.

Ibid.

How else is one to begin again, save by re-finding one's
virginity? And when one finds one's virginity, one realises one
is among the gods.   *Ibid.* (Kate)

The ancient mystery of the female power consists in glorifying
the blood-male.

Ibid.

Man is a column of blood, with a voice in it. And when the
voice is still, and he is only a column of blood, he is better.
Ibid. (Don Ramón)

How wonderful sex can be, when men keep it powerful and
sacred, and it fills the world! Like sunshine through and
through.

Ibid. (Kate)

With the fall of the individual, sex falls into a dog's heat …
Dogs are social beings, with no true canine individuality.
Wolves and foxes don't copulate on the pavement. Their sex is
wild and in act utterly private. Howls you may hear, but you
will never see anything. But the dog is tame – and he makes
excrement and he copulates on the pavement, as if to spite you.

'John Galsworthy', 1927

One has to fight, but not in the O Glory! sort of way. I feel one
still has to fight for the phallic reality, as against the
non-phallic cerebration unrealities.

Letter to Witter Brynner, 1928

There is a hidden will behind all theories of sex, implacable.
And that is the will to deny, to wipe out the mystery of beauty.

'Sex versus Loveliness', 1928

Society has a mysterious hatred of sex, because it perpetually
interferes with the nice money-making schemes of social man.

Ibid.

Sex appeal is only a dirty name for a bit of life-flame. No man
works so well and so successfully as when some woman has
kindled a little fire in his veins.

Ibid.

The real trouble about women is that they must always go on
trying to adapt themselves to men's theories of women …
When a woman is hysterical it's because she doesn't quite
know what picture of woman to live up to.

'Give Her a Pattern', 1928

The worst part of it is, as soon as a woman really has lived up
to a man's pattern the man dislikes her for it … Whatever the
pattern the poor woman tries to live up to, he'll want another.
And that's the condition of modern marriage.

Ibid.

Modern woman isn't really a fool. But modern man is … He
makes a greater mess of his women than men have ever made.
Because he absolutely does not know *what* he wants her to be.

Ibid.

The whole trouble with sex is that we daren't speak of it and think of it naturally. We are not secretly sexual villains. We are not secretly sexually depraved. We are just human beings with living sex. We are all right, if we had not this disastrous *fear*.

'The State of Funk', 1928

If I can really sympathise with a woman in her sexual self, it is just a form of warm-heartedness and compassionateness, the most natural life-flow in the world. And it may be a woman of seventy-five, or a child of two, it is the same.

Ibid.

If there is one thing I don't like it is cheap and promiscuous sex. If there is one thing I insist on it is that sex is a delicate, vulnerable, vital thing that you mustn't fool with … not a trick thing, or a moment's excitation, or a mere bit of bullying.

Ibid.

It is curious what a subtle but unmistakable transmutation [sex] makes, both in the body of men and women: the woman more blooming, more subtly rounded, her young angularities softened, and her expression either anxious or triumphant: the man much quieter, more inward, the very shapes of his shoulders and his buttocks less assertive, more hesitant.

Lady Chatterley's Lover, 1928

I believe in being warm-hearted. I believe especially in being warm-hearted in love, in fucking with a warm heart. I believe if men could fuck with warm hearts, and the women would take it warm-heartedly, everything would come all right. It's all this cold-hearted fucking that is death and idiocy.

Ibid. (Mellors)

Sex is really only touch, the closest of all touch. And it's touch we're afraid of. We're only half-conscious, and half-alive. We've got to come alive and aware. Especially the English have got to get in touch with one another, a bit delicate and a bit tender. It's our crying need.

Ibid. (Mellors)

It is so good to be chaste, like a river of cool water in the soul … How can men want wearisomely to philander? What a misery to be like Don Juan, and impotent ever to fuck oneself into peace.

Ibid. (Mellors)

By being wise and scientific in the serious and earnest manner, you only tend to disinfect the dirty little secret, and either kill sex altogether or else leave it miserable ... the unhappy 'free and pure' love of so many.

'Pornography and Obscenity', 1929

The great danger in masturbation lies in its merely exhaustive nature. In sexual intercourse, there is give and take. A new stimulus enters as the native stimulus departs ... But in masturbation there is nothing but loss.   *Ibid.*

A woman hates to feel that she believes in nothing and stands for nothing ... But a man can be a tramp, purposeless, and be happy.   'Nobody Loves Me', 1929

The most egoistic woman is always in a tangle of hate, if not of love. But the true male egoist neither hates nor loves. He is quite empty, at the middle of him.

Ibid.

Women wanted freedom. The result is a hollowness, an emptiness which frightens the stoutest heart. Women then turned to women for love. But that doesn't last. It can't. Whereas the emptiness persists and persists.

Ibid.

The appearance of syphilis in our midst gave a fearful blow to our sexual life. The real natural innocence of Chaucer was impossible after that.

The Paintings of D.H. Lawrence, 1929 (Introduction)

To-day [is] the great day of the masturbating consciousness, when the mind prostitutes the sensitive responsive body, and produces all kinds of novelties, which thrill for the moment, then go very dead.

Ibid.

The instinct of *fidelity* is perhaps the deepest instinct in the great complex we call sex. Where there is real sex there is the underlying passion for fidelity.

'A Propos of *Lady Chatterley*', 1930

The womb too is the source of life, and a great fountain of dance movements.

Etruscan Places, 1932

Psychology & Self

How to act, that is the question? Whither to go, how to become oneself? One is not oneself, one is merely a half-stated question.

The Rainbow, 1915

It isn't the being that must follow the mind, but the mind must follow the being.

Letter to Middleton Murry, 1916

Nothing in the world is more pernicious than the *ego* or spurious self, the conscious entity with which every individual is saddled. He receives it almost *en bloc* from the preceding generation, and spends the rest of his life trying to drag his spontaneous self from beneath the horrible incubus.

'Democracy', 1917

Your idealist alone is a perfect materialist. This is no paradox. What is an idea, or the ideal, after all? It is only a fixed, static entity … an extraction from the living body. *Ibid.*

Our life, our being depends on the incalculable issue from a central Mystery into indefinable *presence.* This sounds in itself an abstraction. But not so. It is rather the perfect absence of abstraction. The central Mystery is each man's primal original soul or self, within him. *Ibid.*

The living self has one purpose only: to come into its own fullness of being, as a tree comes into full blossom, or a bird into spring beauty, or a tiger into lustre … The only thing man has to trust to in coming to himself is his desire and his impulse. *Ibid.*

I wish one could cease to be a human being, and be a demon. *Allzu Menschlich.*

Letter to Katherine Mansfield, 1919

The be-all and end-all of life doesn't lie in happiness. Happiness is a sort of soap-tablet … Could anything be more puerile than a mankind howling because it isn't happy: like a baby in the bath!

The Lost Girl, 1920

It is not only the prophet who hath honour *save* in his own
country: it is everyone with individuality.   *Ibid.*

You've got to lapse out before you can know what sensual
reality is, lapse into unknowingness, and give up your own
volition ... You've got to learn not-to-be, before you can come
into being.   *Women in Love*, 1921 (Birkin)

You can only have knowledge, strictly, of things concluded, in
the past. It's like bottling the liberty of last summer in the
bottled gooseberries.

Ibid. (Birkin)

One is ill because one doesn't live properly – can't. It's the
failure to live that makes one ill, and humiliates one.

Ibid. (Birkin)

The ego is merely the sum total of what we conceive ourselves
to be. The powerful pristine subjectivity of the unconscious on
its first plane is, on the other hand ... something quite different
[and] the root of all our consciousness.

Psychoanalysis and the Unconscious, 1921

Blessed is he who expecteth nothing, for he shall not be
disappointed.   *Sea and Sardinia*, 1921

It is the reckless blood which achieves all, the piff-piff-piffing
of the mental and moral intelligence is but a subsidiary help, a
mere instrument.   *Ibid.*

In the sun men are objective, in the mist and snow, subjective.
Subjectivity is largely a question of the thickness of your
overcoat.   'Giovanni Verga', 1922

Only at his maximum does an individual surpass all his
derivative elements and become purely himself.

Fantasia of the the Unconscious, 1922

The more you reach after the fatal flower of happiness, which
trembles so blue and lovely in a crevice just beyond your
grasp, the more fearfully you become aware of the ghastly and
awful gulf of the precipice below you, into which you will
inevitably plunge, as into the bottomless pit, if you reach any
farther.

The Fox, 1922

A Jesus makes a Judas inevitable. A man should remain himself, not try to spread himself over humanity. He should pivot himself on his own pride.

Aaron's Rod, 1922 (Lilly)

Mankind loves being impressed. It asks to be impressed. It almost forces those whom it can force to play a role and to make an impression. And afterwards, never forgives.

Ibid. (Lilly)

Men are not free when they are doing just what they like … Men are only free when they are doing what the deepest self likes … We are only free so long as we obey.

Studies in Classic American Literature, 1923 (Spirit of Place)

Beware of absolutes. There are many gods.

Ibid. (Franklin)

Don't be too clean. It impoverishes the blood.

Ibid. (Franklin)

Absolutely the safest thing to get your emotional reactions over is NATURE… [But] this Nature-sweet-and-pure business is only another effort at intellectualizing. Just an attempt to make all nature succumb to a few laws of the human mind.

Ibid. (de Crèvecoeur)

If a man feels superior, he should have it out with himself. 'Do I feel superior because I *am* superior? Or is it just the snobbishness of class, or education, or money?' Class, education, money won't make a man superior. But if he is just *born* superior, in himself, there it is.

Ibid. (Cooper)

It is easy to see why each man kills the thing he loves. To *know* a living thing is to kill it. You have to kill a thing to know it satisfactorily. For this reason, the desirous consciousness, the SPIRIT, is a vampire.

Ibid. (Poe)

When the self is broken, and the mystery of recognition of *otherness* fails, then the longing for identification with the beloved becomes a lust.

Ibid. (Poe)

The lust of hate is the inordinate desire to consume and unspeakably possess the soul of the hated one, just as the lust of love is the desire to possess, or to be possessed by, the beloved utterly. *Ibid.* (Poe)

The harder a man works, at brute labour, the thinner becomes his idealism, the darker his mind. And the harder a man works, at mental labour, at idealism, at transcendental occupations, the thinner becomes his blood, and the more brittle his nerves.

Ibid. (Hawthorne)

KNOWING and BEING are opposite, antagonistic states. The more you know, exactly, the less you *are* ... This is the great cross of man ... Knowing is the slow death of being.

Ibid. (Dana)

I would rather be flogged than have most people 'like' me. *Ibid.* (Dana)

The soul is neither 'above' nor 'within'. It is a wayfarer down the open road. *Ibid.* (Whitman)

There are, in the consciousness of man, two bodies of knowledge; the things he tells himself, and the things he finds out. The things he tells himself are nearly always pleasant, and they are lies. The things he finds out are usually rather bitter to begin with. 'Books', 1924

The blood also thinks, inside a man, darkly and ponderously. It thinks in desires and revulsions, and it makes strange conclusions ... My bood tells me there is no such thing as perfection. There is the long endless venture into consciousness down an ever-dangerous valley of days.

Ibid.

If anatomy presupposes a corpse, then psychology presupposes a world of corpses. If you cut a thing up, of course it will smell. Hence, nothing raises such an infernal stink, at last, as human psychology.

St Mawr, 1925

It's just as great a mistake to laugh at everything as to cry at everything. Laughter's not the one panacea, either.

Ibid. (Mrs Witt)

Those who are born cowed are natural slaves, and deep instinct makes them fear with poisonous fear those who might suddenly snap the slave's collar round their necks.

The Virgin and the Gypsy, 1925

Time is, after all, only the current of the soul in its flow.

Ibid.

Give me a little splendour, and I'll leave perfection to the small fry.   'Accumulated Mail', 1925

Men and women have incomplete selves, made up of bits assembled together loosely and somewhat haphazard. Man was not created ready-made.

The Plumed Serpent, 1926

Brief contacts are all right, thrilling even. But close contacts are short and long revulsions of violent disgust.   *Ibid.*

Man is a creature who wins his own creation inch by inch from the nest of the cosmic dragons. Or else he loses it little by little, and goes to pieces.   *Ibid.* (Don Ramón)

Those that want to be ravished are parasites on the soul ... Those that want to ravish are vampires.

Ibid. (Don Ramón)

If one tries to be unlimited, one becomes horrible.

Ibid. (Kate)

In the core of the first of suns, whence man draws his vitality, lies poison as bitter as the rattlesnake's. This poison man must overcome, he must be master of its issue.

Mornings in Mexico, 1927

Sentimentalism is the working off on yourself of feelings you haven't really got ... Faked feelings! The world is all gummy with them. They are better than real feelings, because you can spit them out when you brush your teeth; and then to-morrow you can fake them afresh.

'John Galsworthy', 1927

I am weary even of my own individuality, and simply nauseated by other people's.

Letter to Dr Trigant Burrow, 1927

What could show a more poisoned hatred of sex than Freudian psycho-analysis?

'Sex versus Loveliness', 1928

Most of the matters of ordinary life ... how you make your money, or whether you love your wife, or if you have 'affairs' ... concern only the person concerned and, like going to the privy, have no interest for anyone else.

Lady Chatterley's Lover, 1928

It's no good trying to get rid of your own aloneness. You've got to stick to it all your life. Only at times, at times, the gap will be filled in ... But you have to wait for the times ... And accept the times when the gap is filled in.

Ibid.

The root of sanity is in the balls.

Ibid. (Mellors)

An independent income is the only thing that never lets you down.

Ibid. (Connie's father)

In his adventure of self-consciousness a man must come to the limits of himself and become aware of something beyond him.

'Pornography and Obscenity', 1929

Every time you force your feelings, you damage yourself and produce the opposite effect to the one you want. Try to force yourself to love somebody, and you are bound to end by detesting that same somebody.

'Nobody Loves Me', 1929

What you *intuitively* desire, that is possible to you. Whereas what you mentally or 'consciously' desire is nine times out of ten impossible: hitch your wagon to a star, and you'll just stay where you are.

The Paintings of D.H. Lawrence, 1929 (Introduction)

Man can have the serpent with him or against him. When his serpent is with him, he is almost divine. When his serpent is against him, he is stung and envenomed and defeated from within.

Apocalypse, 1930

Travel & Places

I would like to go to a land where there are only birds and beasts and no humanity, nor inhumanity-masks.

Letter to Cynthia Asquith, 1915

If only nations would realise that they have certain natural characteristics, if only they could understand and agree to each other's particular nature, how much simpler it would all be.

Twilight in Italy, 1916

When one walks, one must travel west or south. If one turns northward or eastward it is like walking down a cul-de-sac, to the blind end.

Ibid.

Whatever life may be, and whatever horror men have made of it, the world is a lovely place, a magic place, something to marvel over. The world is an amazing place.

The Lost Girl, 1920 (Alvina)

How thankful one can be, to be out of one's country ... I am transported, the moment I set foot on a foreign shore. I say to myself: 'Here steps a new creature into life.'

Women in Love, 1921 (Gudrun)

Paris, no! Between the *religion d'amour*, and the latest 'ism, and the new turning to Jesus, one had better ride on a carousel all day.

Ibid. (Loerke)

Ah, God, liberty, liberty, elemental liberty. I wished in my soul the voyage might last forever, that the sea had no end, that one might float in this wavering, tremulous, yet long and surging pulsation while ever time lasted: space never exhausted, and no turning back, no looking back, even.

Sea and Sardinia, 1921

It is much nicest, on the whole, to travel third-class on the railway. There is space, there is air, and it is like being in a lively inn, everybody in good spirits.

Ibid.

Room – give me room – give me room for my spirit: and you
can have all the toppling crags of romance.   *Ibid.*

Strange is a Celtic landscape, far more moving, disturbing,
than the lovely glamour of Italy and Greece. Before the
curtains of history lifted, one feels the world was like this – this
Celtic bareness and sombreness and *air*. But … I believe there
were never any Celts, as a race.   *Ibid.*

To tell the truth, strangers are not popular nowadays – not
anywhere. Everybody has a grudge against them at first sight.
          Ibid.

How wonderful it must have been to Ulysses to venture into
this Mediterranean and open his eyes on all the loveliness of
the tall coasts. How marvellous to steal with his ship into these
magic harbours. There is something eternally morning-
glamourous about these lands as they rise from the sea. And it
is always the *Odyssey* which comes back to one as one looks at
them. All the lovely morning-wonder of this world, in Homer's
day!   *Ibid.*

Sights are an irritating bore.   *Ibid.*

The East is not for me – the sensuous spiritual voluptuousness,
the curious sensitiveness of the naked people, their black
bottomless, hopeless eyes … Altogether the topics have
something of the world before the flood – hot dark mud and
the life inherent in it: makes me feel rather sick.
          Letter to Cynthia Asquith, 1922

If you want to know what it is to feel the 'correct' social world
fizzle to nothing, you should come to Australia. It *is* a weird
place. In the *established* sense, it is socially nil. Happy-go-lucky,
don't-you-bother, we're-in-Australia. But also there seems to
be no inside life of any sort: just a long lapse and drift. A rather
fascinating indifference, a *physical* indifference to what we call
soul or spirit … It would be a lovely country to lose the world
in altogether.   Letter to Catherine Carswell, 1922

Perhaps it is necessary for me to try these places, perhaps it is
my destiny for me to know the world. It only excites the
outside of me. The inside it leaves more isolated and stoic than
ever … It is all a form of running away from oneself and the
great problems.   *Ibid.*

Men are free when they are in a living homeland ... when they are obeying some deep, inward voice of religious belief ... when they belong to a living, organic, *believing* community ... Not when they are escaping to some wild west. The most unfree souls go west, and shout of freedom.

Studies in Classic American Literature, 1923 (Spirit of Place)

At a certain point, human life becomes uninteresting to men. What then? They turn to some universal. The greatest material mother of us all is the sea.

Ibid. (Dana)

One doesn't talk any more about being happy – that is child's talk. But I do like having the big, unbroken spaces round me. There is something savage, unbreakable in the spirit of place out here [in New Mexico].

Letter to Catherine Carswell, 1924

Something about the Germanic races is unalterable. White-skinned, elemental, and dangerous.

'A Letter from Germany', 1924

Germany freezes my insides, and does something to my chest.

'The Border-Line', 1924

To go South! Always to go South, away from the arctic horror as far as possible! ... To go out of the clutch of greyness and low skies, of sweeping rain, and of slow, blanketing snow. Never again to feel the idealistic, Christianized tension of the now irreligious North.   *St Mawr*, 1925

I begin to hate journeys – I've journeyed enough.

Letter to Rolf Gardiner, 1926

North of the Alps, the everlasting winter is interrupted by summers that struggle and soon yield; south of the Alps, the everlasting summer is interrupted by spasmodic and spiteful winters that never get a real hold.   'Flowery Tuscany', 1926

Superficially, the world has become small and known. Poor little globe of earth, the tourists trot round you as easily as they trot round the Bois or round Central Park. There is no mystery left, we've been there, we've seen it, we know all about it. We've done the globe, and the globe is done ... Yet the more we know, superficially, the less we penetrate, vertically.

'New Mexico', 1928

I shall never be well any more in Europe – so dead! Nothing to re-act to.

Letter to Maria and Aldous Huxley, 1928

I am thankful to God to escape anything like a permanency. 'Better fifty years of Europe than a cycle of Cathay'. Well, I've had nearly fifty years of Europe, so I should rather try the cycle of Cathay.

Ibid., 1929

England

England is only a spot of grease on the soup just now.

Letter to Cynthia Asquith, 1913

London seems to me like some hoary massive underworld, a hoary ponderous inferno. The traffic flows through the rigid grey streets like the rivers of hell through their banks of dry, rocky ash.

Letter to Ottoline Morrell, 1915

Wherein are we superior [to the Mediterranean races]? Only because we went beyond the phallus in search of the Godhead, the creative origin, and we found the physical forces and the secrets of science.

We have exalted Man far above the man who is in each one of us ... But we have exhausted ourselves in the process.

Twilight in Italy, 1916

It isn't a question of nations. France is far worse.

Women in Love, 1921 (Birkin)

Don't be too hard on poor old England. Though we curse it, we love it really ... But it's a damnably uncomfortable love: like a love for an aged parent who suffers horribly from a complication of diseases, for which there is no hope.

Ibid. (Gerald and Birkin)

Nationally all Englishmen must die, so that they can exist individually.

Ibid. (Birkin)

The Italians are not to blame for their spite against us. We, England, have taken upon ourselves for so long the role of leading nation. And if you take upon yourself to lead, you must expect the mud to be thrown at you if you lead into a nasty morass.   *Ibid.*

It is remarkable how many odd or extraordinary people there are in England. We hear continual complaints of the stodgy dullness of the English. It would be quite as just to complain of their freakish, unusual characters.   *Aaron's Rod*, 1922

Why is it, do you think, that English people abroad go so very *queer* – so ultra-English – *incredible!* – and at the same time so perfectly impossible? ... As for their sexual behaviour ... all quite flagrant, quite unabashed – under the cover of this fanatical Englishness.   *Ibid.* (Francis)

Nearly all people in England are of the superior sort, superiority being an English ailment.

'The Last Laugh', 1924

Every Englishman, especially of the upper classes, has a wholesome respect for riches. But then, who hasn't?

St Mawr, 1925

The first half-hour in London, after some years abroad, is really a plunge of misery.

'Dull London', 1928

England can afford to be so free and individual because no individual flame of life is sharp and vivid. It is just mildly warm and safe.   *Ibid.*

My deepest private dread of London is dread of talk ... I feel like a spider whose thread has been caught by somebody, and is being drawn out of him, so he must spin, spin, spin, and all to no purpose ... Talk for talk's sake, without the very faintest intention of a result in action.

Ibid.

Any true-born English gentleman would scorn to let such a thing [as] a grudge and a grievance appear blatant in his own demeanour.

Lady Chatterley's Lover, 1928

England of today is producing a new race of mankind, over-conscious in the money and social and political side, on the spontaneous, intuitive side dead, but dead. Half-corpses, all of them: but with a terrible insistent consciousness in the other half. There is something uncanny and underground about it all. It is an underworld.

Ibid.

The English have delighted in landscape, and have succeeded in it well. It is a form of escape for them, from the actual human body they so hate and fear, and it is an outlet for their perishing aesthetic desires.

The Paintings of D.H. Lawrence, 1929 (Introduction)

The real tragedy of England, as I see it, is the tragedy of ugliness. The country is so lovely: the man-made England is so vile.

'Nottingham and the Mining Country', 1929

The English are town-birds through and through, to-day, as the inevitable result of their complete industrialization. Yet they don't know how to build a city, how to think of one, or how to live in one. They are all suburban, pseudo-cottage ... There *is* no Nottingham, in the sense that there is Siena.

Ibid.

The young Englishmen fill me with savage despair – so without fire, without spark, without spunk – so *ineffectual.* What's the good of such people, though they are clever? They think the whole end of living is achieved if they talk, with a drink, rather amusingly and cleverly for an evening.

Letter to Maria and Aldous Huxley, 1929

Italy

The Italian people are called 'Children of the Sun'. They might better be called 'Children of the Shadow'. Their souls are dark and nocturnal. If they are to be easy, they must be able to hide, to be hidden in lairs and caves of darkness.

Twilight in Italy, 1916

The secret of Italy's attraction for us [is] phallic worship. To the Italian the phallus is the symbol of individual creative immortality, to each man his own Godhead. The child is but evidence of the Godhead.

Ibid.

Death has no beauty in Italy, unless it be violent. The death of a man or woman through sickness is an occasion of horror, repulsive. They belong entirely to life, they are so limited to life, these people.

Ibid.

The substratum of Italy has always been pagan, sensuous, the
most potent symbol the sexual symbol. The child is really a
non-Christian symbol: it is the symbol of man's triumph of
eternal life in procreation. The worship of the Cross never
really held good in Italy. The Christianity of Northern Europe
has never had any place there.   *Ibid.*

In Italy, there is no escape. Say two words, and the individual
starts chewing old newspaper and stuffing it into you. You
become – if you are English – *l'Inghilterra, il carbone,* and *il
cambio;* and as England, coal, and exchange you are treated. It
is more than useless to try to be human about it.

Sea and Sardinia, 1921

Italy is so tender – like cooked macaroni – yards and yards of
soft tenderness ravelled round everything.   *Ibid.*

Italian landscape is really eighteenth-century landscape, to be
represented in that romantic-classic manner which makes
everything rather marvellous and very topical: aqueducts, and
ruins upon sugar-loaf mountains, and craggy ravines and
Wilhelm Meister waterfalls, all up and down.

Ibid.

To *penetrate* into Italy is like a most fascinating act of
self-discovery – back, back down the old ways of time. Strange
and wonderful chords awake in us, and vibrate again after
many hundreds of years of complete forgetfulness … And then
– and then – there is a final feeling of sterility. It is all worked
out. It is all known: *connu, connu!*

Ibid.

Never was such a language of sympathy as the Italian.
Poverino! Poverino! They are never happy unless they are
sympathising pityingly with somebody.

Ibid.

I like Italian newspapers because they say what they mean,
and not merely what is most convenient to say. We call it
naiveté – I call it manliness. Italian newpapers read as if they
were written by men, and not by calculating eunuchs.

Ibid.

The Italian good-nature forms a sound and unshakable basis
nowadays for their extortion and self-justification and spite.

Ibid.

The look of a man who does not think, but whose heart is all
the time red hot with burning, generous blood-passion. This is
what [the Italians] adore.

Ibid.

All Italy, apart from the plains, is a hanging garden ... It is a
work of many, many centuries ... Man, feeling his way
sensitively to the fruitfulness of the earth, has moulded the
earth to his necessity without violating it. Which shows
that man *can* live on the earth and by the earth without
disfiguring it.

'Flowery Tuscany', 1926

The Italians are not passionate: passion has deep reserves.
They are easily moved, and often affectionate, but they rarely
have any abiding passion of any sort.

Lady Chatterley's Lover, 1928

America

[Italian] men must go away to America. It is not the money. It
is the profound desire to rehabilitate themselves, to recover
some dignity as men, as producers, as workers, as creators
from the spirit, not only from the flesh. It is a profound desire
to get away from women altogether, the terrible subjugation to
sex, the phallic worship.

Twilight in Italy, 1916

All these naive Americans – they are a good deal older and
shrewder than we, once it nears the point. And they seem to
feel as if the world were coming to an end. And they are so
truly generous of their hospitality in this cold world.

Sea and Sardinia, 1921

In [America], everything is taken so damn seriously that
nothing remains serious. Nothing is so farcical as insistent
drama.

'Indians and an Englishman', 1922

Americans refuse everything explicit and always put up a sort
of double meaning. They revel in subterfuge.

Studies in Classic American Literature, 1923

Free? Why, I have never been in any country where the
individual has such an abject fear of his fellow countrymen.

Ibid. (Spirit of Place)

A vast republic of escaped slaves ... And a minority of earnest, self-tortured people.

Ibid. (Spirit of Place)

First and foremost, [the Yankees] hated masters. But under that, they hated the flowing ease of humour in Europe. At the bottom of the American soul was always a dark suspense [which] hated and hates the old European spontaneity [and] watches it collapse with satisfaction.

Ibid. (Spirit of Place)

Democracy in America is just the tool with which the old master of Europe, the European spirit, is undermined. Europe destroyed, potentially, American democracy will evaporate. America will begin.

Ibid. (Spirit of Place)

All this Americanizing and mechanizing has been for the purpose of overthrowing the past. And now look at America, tangled in her own barbed wire ... Now is your chance, Europe. Now let Hell loose and get your own back.

Ibid. (Franklin)

In the Land of the Free, the greatest delight of every man is in getting the better of the other man.

Ibid. (de Crèvecoeur)

The most idealist nations invent most machines. America simply teems with mechanical inventions, because nobody in America ever wants to *do* anything. They are idealists. Let a machine do the doing.

Ibid. (de Crèvecoeur)

European decadence was anticipated in America ... Baudelaire learned his lesson from [Poe].

Ibid. (Cooper)

There are more ways than one of vandalism. I should think the American admiration of five-minute tourists has done more to kill the sacredness of old European beauty and aspiration than multitudes of bombs would have done.

Ibid. (Cooper)

There'll never be any life in America till you pull the pin out and admit natural inequality.

Ibid. (Cooper)

It is perhaps easier to love America passionately, when you look at it through the wrong end of the telescope, across all the Atlantic water ... When you are actually *in* America, America hurts, because it has a powerful disintegrative influence upon the white psyche. *Ibid.* (Cooper)

Democracy in America was never the same as Liberty in Europe. In Europe Liberty was the great life-throb. But in America Democracy was always something anti-life ... American democracy was a form of self-murder always.

Ibid. (Cooper)

There is always a certain slightly devilish resistance in the American landscape.

Ibid. (Cooper)

The essential American soul is hard, isolate, stoic, and a killer. It has never yet melted. *Ibid.* (Cooper)

The deliberate consciousness of Americans [is] so fair and smooth-spoken, and the under-consciousness so devilish. *Destroy! destroy! destroy!* hums the under-consciousness. *Love and produce! Love and produce!* cackles the upper-consciousness. *Ibid.* (Hawthorne)

It is [the American's] destiny to destroy the whole corpus of the white psyche, the white consciousness. And he's got to do it secretly. *Ibid.* (Hawthorne)

In America, nobody does anything from the blood. Always from the nerves, if not from the mind.

Ibid. (Hawthorne)

Americans have never loved the soil of America as Europeans have loved the soil of Europe. America has never been a blood home-land. Only an ideal homeland ... That has yet to come. *Ibid.* (Dana)

Transcendentalism. Transcend this home-land business, exalt the idea of these States till you have made it a universal idea, says the true American. The over-soul is a world-soul, not a local thing.

Ibid. (Dana)

The best Americans are mystics by instinct. *Ibid.* (Dana)

Typically American: doing the most impossible things without taking off their spiritual get-up. Their ideals are like armour which has rusted on, and will never more come off.

Ibid. (Melville)

The American heroic message: the soul is not to pile up defences round herself. She is not to withdraw and seek her heavens inwardly, in mystical ecstasies. She is not to cry to some God beyond, for salvation. She is to go down the open road, accomplishing nothing save the journey, and the works incidental to the journey.

Ibid. (Whitman)

Americans despair of having lived in vain, or of not having *really* lived. Having missed something. Which fearful misgiving makes them rush like mechanical steel filings to a magnet, towards any crowd in the street.

The Plumed Serpent, 1926

The cult of the dollar is far more intense in the countries that haven't got the dollar.

Ibid.

The real insanity of America is the automobile. As men used to want a horse and a sword, now they want a car. As women used to pine for a home and a box at the theatre, now it is a 'machine'.   *Ibid.*

The tremendous potent elements of the American continent give men powerful bodies, but weigh the soul down and prevent its rising into birth. Or, if a man arrives with a soul, the maleficent elements gradually break it … till he decomposes into ideas and mechanistic activities.

Ibid.

The Mediterranean, so eternally young, the very symbol of youth! And Italy, so reputedly old, yet forever so child-like and naive! Never, never for a moment able to comprehend the wonderful, hoary age of America, the continent of the afterwards.   *Mornings in Mexico*, 1927

It is curious that the land which has produced modern political democracy at its highest pitch should give one the greatest sense of overweening, terrible proudness and mercilessness: but so beautiful, God! so beautiful!

'New Mexico', 1928

Mexico

Mexico has an underlying ugliness, a sort of squalid evil,
which makes Naples seem debonair in comparison.

The Plumed Serpent, 1926

There are so many shady people in Mexico that it is taken for
granted, if you arrive unannounced and unexpected in the
capital, that you are probably under an assumed name, and
have some dirty game up your sleeve.

Ibid.

When they forget all about the Patria and Mexico and all that
stuff, [the Mexicans] are as nice a people as you'd find.

Ibid. (Henry)

What men call liberty here is just freedom to commit crime.

Ibid. (Judge Burlap)

Superficially, Mexico might be all right: with its suburbs of
villas, its central fine streets, its thousands of motorcars, its
tennis, and its bridge-parties. The sun shines brilliantly
everyday, and big bright flowers stand out from the trees. It is
a holiday. Until you [are] alone with it. And then the
undertone is like the low, angry, snarling purring of some
jaguar spotted with night ... The spirit of place is cruel,
down-dragging, destructive.

Ibid.

No man who hasn't a strong moral backbone should try to
settle in Mexico. If he does, he'll go to pieces ... as hundreds of
young Americans do.

Ibid. (an old American)

There is passionate life [in Mexico]. But nowhere is there any
sign of energy. This is, as it were, switched off.

Ibid.

In Mexico it is a crime to be rich, or to be classed with the rich.
Not even a crime, really, so much as a freak. The rich class is a
freak class, like dogs with two heads or calves with five legs.

Ibid.

Religion & Transcendence

To be rid of our individuality, which is our will, which is our effort – to live effortless, a kind of conscious sleep – that is very beautiful, I think; that is our after-life – our immortality.

Sons and Lovers, 1913 (Paul)

The Resurrection [should be] to life, not to death. Shall I not see those who have risen again walk here among men perfect in body and spirit, whole and glad in the flesh, living in the flesh, loving in the flesh, begetting children in the flesh, arrived at last to wholeness, perfect without scar or blemish, healthy without fear of ill-health?

The Rainbow, 1915

Religion is but a particular clothing to a human aspiration. The aspiration is the real thing, – the clothing is a matter almost of national taste or need. The Greeks had a naked Apollo, the Christians a white-robed Christ, the Buddhists a royal prince, the Egyptians their Osiris. Religions are local and religion is universal. Christianity is a local branch. There is as yet no assimilation of local religions into universal religion.

Ibid.

Where is the supreme ecstasy in mankind, which makes day a delight and night a delight, purpose an ecstasy and a concourse in ecstasy, and single abandon of the single body and soul an ecstasy under the moon? Where is the transcendental knowledge in our hearts, uniting sun and darkness, day and night, spirit and senses? Why do we not know the two in consummation are one; that each is only part; partial and alone for ever; but that two in consummation are perfect, beyond the range of loneliness or solitude?

Twilight in Italy, 1916

The senses are the absolute, the god-like ... These are me ... And all that is can only come to me through my senses.

Ibid.

God is that which is Not-Me ... This is the Christian truth, a truth complementary to the Pagan affirmation: 'God is that which is Me.'

Ibid.

Children are not the future. The living truth is the future.
Ibid.

It is all very well to talk about a Supreme Being, an Anima Mundi, an Oversoul, an Infinite: but it is all just human invention. Come down to actuality. Where do you see Being? – In individual men and women.   *'Democracy', 1917*

The universe contains no tragedy, and man is only tragical because he is afraid of death. For my part, if the sun always shines, and always will shine, in spite of millions of clouds of words, then death, somehow, does not have many terrors. In the sunshine, even death is sunny. And there is no end to sunshine.   *Ibid.*

If Jesus had paid more attention to Magdalene, and less to his disciples, it would have been better. It was not the ointment-pouring which was so devastating, but the discipleship of the twelve.   Letter to Cecil Gray, 1918

Oh, I wish he would *stand up*!
On Seeing a Statue of the Buddha, 1922

The dead don't die. They look on and help.
Letter to Middleton Murry, 1923

The Perfectibility of Man! Ah heaven, what a dreary theme!
Studies in Classic American Literature, 1923 (Franklin)

The Holy Ghost bids us never be too deadly in our earnestness, always to laugh in time, at ourselves and everything.
Ibid. (Poe)

The next era is the era of the Holy Ghost. And the Holy Ghost speaks individually inside every individual ... There is no manifestation to the general world.   *Ibid.* (Poe)

The birth of sin was not *doing* it, but KNOWING about it.
Ibid. (Hawthorne)

The greatest thrill in life is to bring down the Sacred Saint with a flop into the mud.   *Ibid.* (Hawthorne)

Sin isn't the breaking of divine commandments. It is the breaking of one's own integrity.   *Ibid.* (Hawthorne)

When men want to be supernatural, be sure that something has gone wrong in their natural stuff. More so, even, with a woman.   *Ibid.* (Hawthorne)

Justice is a great and manly thing. Saviourism is a despicable thing.

Ibid. (Dana)

Striving after righteousness only causes your own slow degeneration ... No men are so evil today as the idealists, and no women half so evil as your earnest woman, who feels herself a power for good.

Ibid. (Melville)

Moses wouldn't have valued the famous tablets if they hadn't been ponderous, and millstones round everybody's neck.
Letter to Middleton Murry, 1924

The adventure has gone out of Christianity. We must start on a new venture toward God.

'Books', 1924

Homo sum! a demon who knows nothing of any First Creator who created the universe from his own perfection. *Homo sum!* a man who knows that all creation lives like some great demon inhabiting space, and pulsing with a dual desire, a desire to give himself forth into creation, and a desire to take himself back, in death.

'Climbing down Pisgah', 1924

I would never belong to any club, or trades union, and God's the same to my mind.

St Mawr, 1925 (Lewis)

I do so understand why Jesus said: *Noli me tangere*. Touch me not. I am not yet ascended unto the father. Everything had hurt him so much, wearied him beyond endurance ... Oh, leave me alone, leave me alone! That is all my cry to all the world.
Ibid. (Lou)

There is no almighty loving God. The god here is shaggy as the pine-trees, and as horrible as the lightning ... What nonsense about Jesus and a God of Love, in a place like [New Mexico]. This is more awful and more splendid. I like it better.
Ibid. (Lou)

Something big, bigger than men, bigger than people, bigger than religion … It's my mission to keep myself for the spirit that is wild.

Ibid. (Lou)

In the kingdom of heaven, in the fourth dimension, each soul that achieves a perfect relationship with the cosmos, from its own centre, is perfect, and incomparable. It has no superior. It is a conqueror, and incomparable … The kingdom of heaven is the kingdom of conquerors.

'Reflections on the Death of a Porcupine', 1925

Gods should be iridescent, like the rainbow in the storm … Gods die with the men who have conceived them. But the God-stuff roars eternally, like the sea, with too vast a sound to be heard.

The Plumed Serpent, 1926

God is always God. But man loses his connection with God. And then he can never recover it again, unless some new saviour comes to give him his new connection.

Ibid. (Dona Carlota)

[How can one] bear the contact of commonplace daily things, when one's soul and body have been naked to the cosmos?

Ibid.

The faces of men, and the hearts of men are helpless quicksands. Only in the heart of the cosmos man can look for strength.

Ibid.

The benevolent people, politicians and socialists and so forth, surcharged with pity for living men, in their mouths, but really with hate – the hate of the materialist *have-nots* for the materialist *haves*: they are the Anti-Christ.

Ibid. (Don Ramón)

The mystery is one mystery, but men must see it differently.

Ibid. (Don Ramón)

That which we get from the beyond, we get it alone. The final me that I am, comes from the farthest off … The rest is assembled.

Ibid.

There is only one thing that a man really wants to do, all his life; and that is, to find his way to his God, his Morning Star, and be alone there. *Ibid.*

The Church, instead of helping men, pushes them more and more into a soft, emotional helplessness, with the unpleasant sensuous gratification of feeling themselves victims, victimized, victimized, but at the same time with the lurking sardonic consciousness that in the end a victim is stronger than the victimizer ... Cursed are the falsely meek, for they are inheriting the earth. *Ibid.*

I don't believe in evolution, like a long string hooked on to a First Cause, and being slowly twisted in unbroken continuity through the ages. I prefer to believe in what the Aztecs called Suns: that is, Worlds successively created and destroyed.

Mornings in Mexico, 1927

For the cultural animist the earth's dark centre holds its dark sun, our source of isolated being round which our world coils its folds like a great snake ... The snake lies nearer to the source of potency, the dark, lurking, intense sun at the centre of the earth.

Ibid.

In the oldest religion, everything was alive, not supernaturally but naturally alive. There were only deeper and deeper streams of life, vibrations of life more and more vast ... The whole life-effort of man was to get his life into contact with the elemental life of the cosmos, mountain-life, cloud-life, thunder-life, air-life, earth-life, sun-life. To come into immediate *felt* contact, and so derive energy, power, and a dark sort of joy ... This vast old religion was greater than anything we know: more starkly and nakedly religious.

'New Mexico', 1928

When Jesus refused the devil's money, he left the devil like a Jewish banker, master of the whole situation.

Lady Chatterley's Lover, 1928

[The people] should be alive and frisky, and acknowledge the great god Pan. He's the only god for the masses, forever. The few can go in for higher cults if they like. But let the mass be forever pagan.

Ibid. (Mellors)

At the maximum of our imagination we are religious.
The Paintings of D.H. Lawrence, 1929 (Introduction)

Brought up a Nonconformist as I was, I just was never able to
understand the language of salvation ... It seemed to work out
as getting rather drunk on your own self-importance, and
afterwards coming dismally sober again and being rather
unpleasant.

Ibid.

My very instincts *resent* the Bible.

Apocalypse, 1930

The aristocrats of the Spirit are to find their fulfilment in
self-realisation and service.

Ibid.

Every saint becomes evil once he touches the collective self of
men ... The great saints are for the *individual* only.

Ibid.

Any rule of saints must be horrible. Why? Because the nature
of man is not saintly ... The human heart needs, needs, needs,
splendour, gorgeousness, pride, assumption, glory, and
lordship. Perhaps it needs these even more than it needs love:
at least, even more than bread.

Ibid.

The Bible is so splendidly full of paganisms and therein lies its
greater interest.

Ibid.

The god of the beginning of an era is the evil principle at the
end of that era ... The good potency of the beginning of the
Christian era is now the evil potency of the end.

Ibid.

There is Jesus – but there is also John the Divine. There is
Christian love – and there is Christian envy. The former would
'save' the world – the latter will never be satisfied till it has
destroyed the world ... The Apocalypse is the feet of clay to
the grand Christian image.

Ibid.

Nature & the Life-force

Life is beautiful, so long as it is consuming you. When it is rushing through you, destroying you, life is glorious. It is best to roar away, like a fire with a great draught, white-hot to the last bit. It's when you burn a slow fire and save fuel that life's not worth living.

'A Modern Lover', 1912

Air and cleanliness are the two most important things in this life.

Letter to Cynthia Asquith, 1913

When there is no one to exult with, and the unsatisfied soul must dance and play, then one dances before the Unknown.

The Rainbow, 1915

What does the self, the form of life, matter? Only the living from day to day matters, the beloved existence in the body, rich, peaceful, complete, with no beyond, no further trouble, no further complication.

Ibid.

Death cannot create or destroy. What is, is.

Twilight in Italy, 1916

The infinite is positive and negative. But the average is only neutral.

Ibid.

You can't make an *idea* of the living self: hence it can never become an ideal ... There can be no ideal goal for human life. Any ideal goal means mechanization, materialism, and nullity.

'Democracy', 1917

Where there is life, there is no death.

'Whistling of Birds', 1919

Life, the ever-present, knows no finality, no finished crystallization. The perfect rose is only a running flame ... Herein lies its transcendent liveliness.

New Poems, 1920 (Preface)

Don't give me the infinite or the eternal ... Give me the still, white seething, the incandescence and the coldness of the incarnate moment ... the immediate present, the Now ... This is the quick of Time.

Ibid.

Why should you always be *doing*? It is so plebian. I think it is much better to be really patrician, and to do nothing, but just be oneself, like a walking flower.

Women in Love, 1921 (Ursula)

Man is a mistake, he must go ... I believe in the unseen hosts.

Ibid. (Birkin)

Dissolution rolls on, just as production does. It is a progressive process – and it ends in universal nothing – the end of the world, if you like. But why isn't the end of the world as good as the beginning? ... It means a new cycle of creation.

Ibid. (Birkin)

Better a thousand times take one's chance with death, than accept a life one does not want. But best of all to persist and persist, and persist for ever, till one is satisfied in life.

Ibid.

I hate ecstasy, Dionysic or any other. It's like going round in a squirrel cage.

Ibid. (Birkin)

How stupid anthropomorphism is! ... The universe is non-human, thank God.

Ibid. (Ursula)

One should die quickly, like the Romans, one should be master of one's fate in dying as in living.   *Ibid.*

Why bother! Why strive for a coherent, satisfied life? Why not drift on in a series of accidents – like a picaresque novel?

Ibid.

One should just live anywhere – not have a definite place ... As soon as you get a room, and it is *complete*, you want to run from it ... It is a horrible tyranny of a fixed milieu, where each piece of furniture is a commandment-stone.

Ibid. (Birkin)

There are only two great dynamic urges in *life*: love and power
… We've got to accept the power motive, accept it in deep
responsibility … It is a vast dark source of life and strength in
us now, waiting either to issue into true action, or to burst into
cataclysm … The will-to-power – but not in Nietzsche's sense.
Not intellectual power. Not mental power. Not conscious
will-power. Not even wisdom. But dark, living, fructifying
power.

Aaron's Rod, 1922 (Lilly)

Everything vital, or natural, is unstable, thank God.
Studies in Classic American Literature, 1923 (Dana)

Thunder, the electric force, is the counterpart in the
material-dynamic world of the life-force, the creative mystery,
itself, in the creative world.

Ibid. (Dana)

Leave love and home. Love and home are a deadly illusion …
The crucifixion into humanity is over. Let us go back to the
fierce, uncanny elements: the corrosive vast sea. Or fire.
Ibid. (Melville)

We must make a great swerve in our onward-going life-course
now, to gather up again the savage mysteries. But this does not
mean going back on ourselves.
Ibid. (Melville)

Love is never a fulfilment. Life is never a thing of continuous
bliss. There is no paradise. Fight and laugh and feel bitter and
feel bliss: and fight again. Fight, fight. That is life. Why pin
ourselves down on a paradisal ideal? It is only ourselves we
torture.
Ibid. (Melville)

Life is no fun for a man, without an adventure … And there's
only one left, the venture of consciousness.
'Climbing down Pisgah', 1924

Freedom! Most slaves can't be freed, no matter how you let
them loose. Like domestic animals, they are, in the long run,
more afraid of freedom than of masters: and freed by some
generous master they will at last crawl back to some mean boss.
St Mawr, 1925

Life moves in circles of power and of vividness, and each circle of life only maintains its orbit upon subjection of some lower circle. If the lower cycles of life are not *mastered*, there can be no higher cycle.

'Reflections on the Death of a Porcupine', 1925

I don't take myself seriously, except between 8.0 and 10.0 a.m., and at the stroke of midnight. At other seasons, my say, like any butterfly, may settle where it likes: on the lily of the field or the horse-tod on the road: or nowhere.

Letter to Middleton Murry, 1926

It is as good as earning money, to have very small expenses.

Letter to Martin Secker, 1926

The longer I live the more loathesome the human species becomes to me.

The Plumed Serpent, 1926 (Kate)

The thing called 'Life' is just a mistake we have made in our own minds. Why persist in the mistake any further?

Ibid.

Give me the mystery and let the world live again for me! ... And deliver me from man's automatism.

Ibid.

Now, and only Now, and forever Now.

Ibid. (Don Ramón)

A quiet, subterranean insolence against life ... seems to belong to modern life. The unbearable note of flippant jeering is underneath almost all modern utterance.

Ibid.

I like the world, the sky and the earth and the greater mystery beyond. But people ... are all monkeys to me ... There is only one way of escape: to turn beyond them, to the greater life.

Ibid. (Don Ramón)

It is life which is the mystery. Death is hardly mysterious in comparison.

Ibid. (Don Ramón)

Tragedy is lack of experience.   'Sun', 1926

The human body is only just coming to real life. With the Greeks it gave a lovely flicker, then Plato and Aristotle killed it, and Jesus finished it off. But now the body is coming really to life, it is really rising from the tomb. And it will be lovely, lovely life in the lovely universe, the life of the human body.

Lady Chatterley's Lover, 1928 (Connie)

One grows more carnal and more mortal as one grows older. Only youth has a taste of immortality.

Ibid. (Clifford)

The world is lovely if one avoids man – so why not avoid him! Why not! Why not! I am tired of humanity.

Letter to Maria and Aldous Huxley, 1929

Oh, be an apple, and leave all your thoughts, all your feelings, all your mind and all your personality, which we know all about and find boring beyond endurance.

The Paintings of D.H. Lawrence, 1929 (Introduction)

We and the cosmos are one. The cosmos is a vast living body, of which we are still parts ... There is an eternal vital correspondence between our blood and the sun: there is an eternal vital correspondence between our nerves and the moon. If we get out of contact and harmony with the sun and moon, then both turn into great dragons of destruction against us.

Apocalypse, 1930

My individualism is really an illusion. I am part of the great whole, and I can never escape. But I *can* deny my connections, break them, and become a fragment. Then I am wretched.

Ibid.

What we want is to destroy our false, inorganic connections, especially those related to money, and re-establish the living organic connections, with the cosmos, the sun and earth, with mankind and nation and family. Start with the sun, and the rest will slowly, slowly happen.

Ibid.